BRIONY HUGHES

Dorothy

I0202321

BROKEN SLEEP BOOKS

All rights reserved; no part of this book
may be reproduced by any means
without the publisher's permission.

Published 2020,
Broken Sleep Books:
Cornwall / Wales

brokensleepbooks.com

The author has asserted their right to be
identified as the author of this Work in
accordance with the Copyright, Designs
and Patents Act 1988

First Edition

Lay out your unrest.

Publisher/Editor: Aaron Kent
Editor: Charlie Baylis

Typeset in UK by Aaron Kent

Broken Sleep Books is committed to
a sustainable future for our planet,
and therefore uses print on
demand publication.

brokensleepbooks@gmail.com

ISBN: 978-1-913642-08-2

Contents

Dorothy is a stunning and crucial intervention into our relationship with water, the Thames River, and the history of Waterloo Bridge. Mediating water through poem, through film, through photograph, body, bath, archive, and even rabbit; Hughes's poignant work acknowledges and disrupts our continual dependence on water, crafting encounters with the River Thames on a colossal and microscopic scale. The visceral diagrammatic and hand drawn shapes connect the structural properties of water to the female body of the poet – a connection that is most keenly felt in its absence; 'via archive' serving as an eloquent reminder of female erasure within this moment of ecological crisis in which water exists as both precious commodity and abundant resource.

  - Cat Chong

Dorothy is a collection of 'via' poems that conveys stories of numberless nameless forgotten women who lived, worked, and died by the river Thames and its tributaries. Briony Hughes locates these women – dripping and drowned in ghastly Victorian poetry; smiling with satisfaction in black and white photographs; brazen in blue overalls during the war effort – restoring their names where possible and paying tribute to their lives. The eponymous Dorothy indicates the 'role official / named only as Dorothy', recently identified by feminist historians in photographs of Waterloo Bridge's builders, one of thousands of women working in the British construction industry in the 1940s. She is, as Hughes writes, 'ankle tied / to cement / blocks', the weight of men's refusal to admit her labour, her strength, her indispensability to capital dragging her down to the murky depths of history. In Hughes's work, she resurfaces in a prismatic burst of bubbles, detritus, and putrefaction.

  Waterloo Bridge is also known as The Ladies Bridge and The Bridge of Sighs. The latter appellation is used by Victorian poet Thomas Hood in a poem of the same name, in which an allegedly poor, pregnant, and outcast woman jumps from the bridge to her death. Hood imagines the woman's body bound in the river as 'the wave constantly / Drips from her clothing' and urges readers to forgive her sins and 'Take her up instantly, / Loving, not loathing – '. In the first poem (or rather, the first textual piece, as the collection begins and ends with drawings and photographs), Hughes salvages language from Hood's poem, channelling dynamism back into the woman's watery grave, allowing words and images to rise and undulate; the poem's stutters, sighs, and gasps accelerating and intensifying as 'clothing the wave the wave clothes'. The influence of Caroline Bergvall – queer feminist adept in utilising the materiality and fluidity of language in order to translate its histories, contexts, and usages – is felt throughout this collection, most keenly in the moments where Hughes develops poetic forms and patterns that function like aqueducts and sewage pipes, conveying readers through historical stuff to the queer feminist horizon of the other side.

Hughes does not attempt to resurrect the tragic woman, or to give her a voice, for we will never know her name let alone hear her speak. But we can think of her; we can learn about the conditions of her life and remember her death apart from the paternalist moralising tone of Hood's poem. 100 years later, the possibilities for women go beyond jumping from that bridge to building it; Dorothy might be understood as an embodiment of those unknown women – those ciphers in poems and photographs – whose lives and deaths must not be relegated to the realm of the unknowable. We follow Hughes, like Adrienne Rich before her, and dive into the wreck. Hughes's poetry is waterlogged in the most fabulously wayward, buoyant, and leaky sense. Down in the depths we might come upon 'globular-bulbous' lifeforms swelling in bubble bath, love-nourished honey rabbits, remedies for political fervour that soothe without subduing any of those rebellious flames. Jump in, the water's dirty!

– Nisha Ramayya

For Laura

Dorothy

Briony Hughes

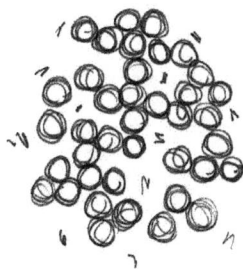

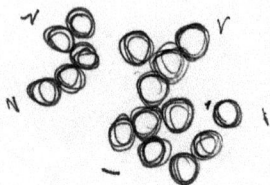

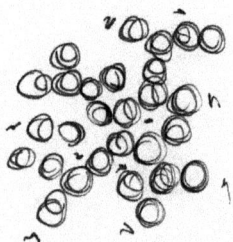

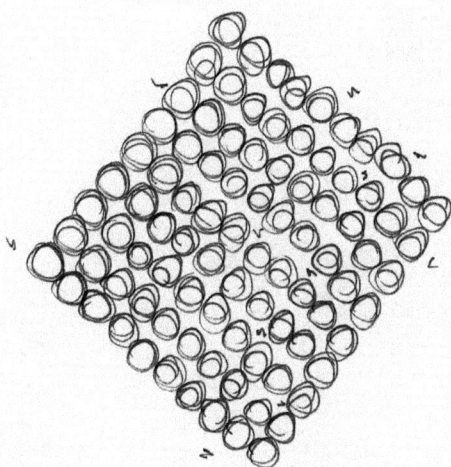

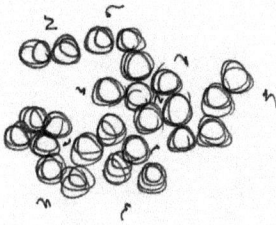

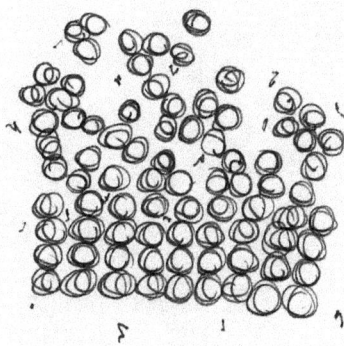

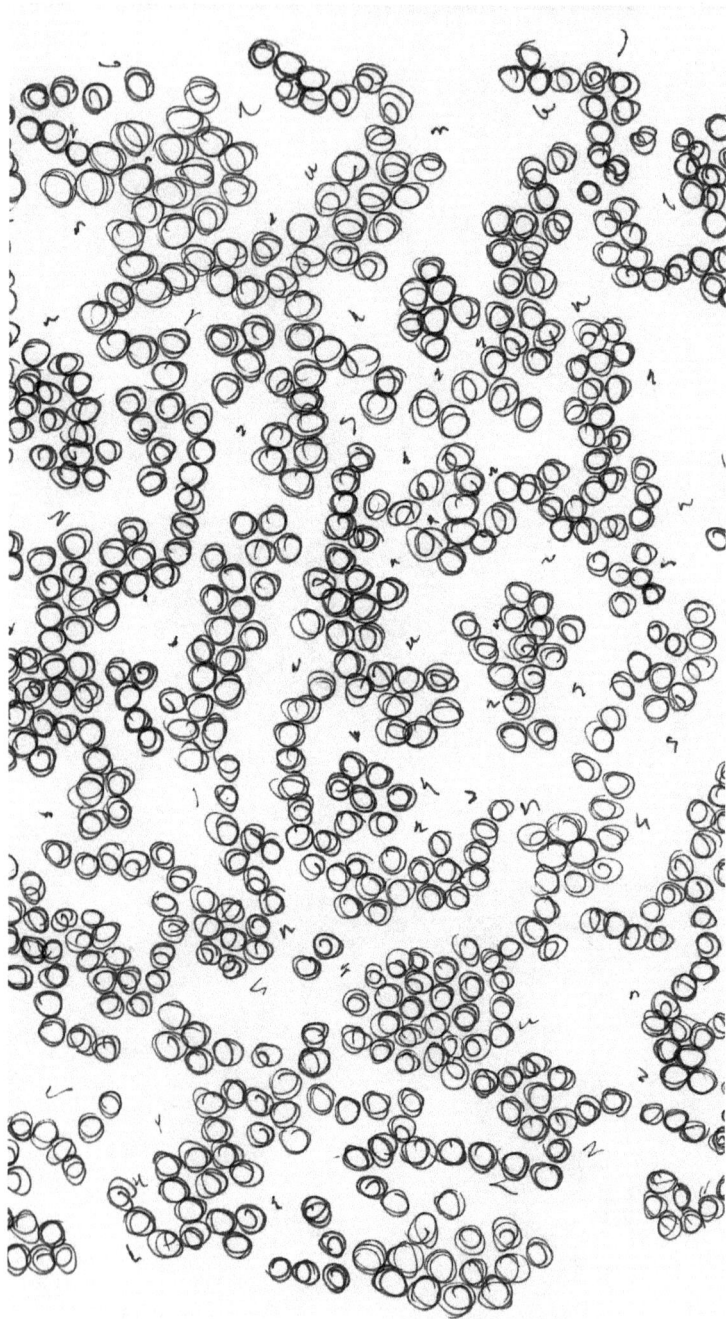

via poem

                                                    the wave
                                                  those waves
                                                waves constant
constantly drip from her
from her clothing those waves drip
      disintegrate   constantly ttt t those waves the wave drips
the drip is constant t t the wave from her
clothing wave dripping those waves
tidal   those drips the clothing
her wave drip
                        sighs
                        those   wave
                        t   the wave
constant wave
constant from her
                by volume   clothing the waves drip
constant constantly constant
her clothing the wave constantly drips
from her clothing clothing the drip drip
      instant   clothing the wave the wave clothes
her clothes her clothing t t   ttt the
drip is constant
the those
                              matter   the the
the wave
the the wave the
constantly drips from her
      without t t ttt t   clothing to clothe the wave the drip
the constant from her waving the   t
      hour   clothing waving the drip the wave
constant from the drip the tt
clothing those
waves t those

via film

old father thames will lose
none   of   his   dignity
through
the   arrival   of   this
newcomer
this lusty child of a new
age

Dorothy   is
ankle   tied
to   cement
blocks   it
will take 73
years
to   t t tt
resurface

via photograph

collected   in
    8-bit   greyscale
           mudlarks
filling those gloves   hands
67
meters from our detritus
wielding
      climate   of

cow teeth dentures clay pipes hypodermic georgian glass
vimto zero sugar alligator prop sex token hot water bottle
samsung ceramic chip windscreen wiper brick glove bike
wheel plastic spoon silver spoon glass bottle plug ball chain key
coin lock thimble dice morrisons trolley everything but name

itself   likely   washed   away   thrown
against   southend
pier into   north   sea   or   channel
where   we
from june to august
        taste her   forming
            tonsil   stones   as
throat stings each sal   t
breath   voicing
her name in our cells or excreted into
                                british
waterways

declared   thames
biologically extinct
maybe her name is with
            the   seals
face-down   rotting   and
 swelling a little
more with each fresh tide

via body

i've   drunk
      one
glass   crushed   lime   fresh
      mint
colour   of   piss   –   £2.85 a
      bottle
the   thames   as   cordial
–   back from
  the   dead   spitting   life   into   the
          sea   –   a   bit
too   strong   –   just   how mum likes it
bring   a
glass a cup a   flask gulp it down and
don't   forget   to wipe   your mouth
or   the water will thicken and the
limescale   from the t ttaps will spread
to your lips and the   creases of
your jaw and your teeth and throat and
nose and eyes and skin   until
you are fully clad in portland stone
and prepared to become a   grade
II   listed   structure –

*there will be no record of this event

via bath

globular-bulbous   as canopy reclines into rosemary
she's shifting against plastic chewed by bodies   froth
and hard water as tangerine into hips slip this breasted retiform brims
thickens skim under the tap   swells across
hot –   furrows and fissures in both
elongated fruit   directions an exchange of
display your tentacles and tube feet!   ripening
rub ginger and active tar against your leather   bark clots at the plug
scalp sifting flickers of white   her foliage reaching across
                                                            a tiled floor

via archives

D   o   r   o   t   h

y   w   a   i   t   s

via rabbit

beside   root   slits

peeled   or   most   likely

gra   ted   unless

delivered   as   a   grass-

lined   subs   trate

syringed   into   throa   t

twice   thrice   daily   after

or   since   I   saw   her   urine

as   t   ributary   soiling   the

basin   ex   tracted   a

runnymede   share   of

thirteen   thousand

until   rinsed   kale

presses   onto   this   ches

t   she   will   not   drink

via transcription

never known it to   the ladies   bridge this was built mainly

female labour   if it wasn't for the ladies this country

 this country would have fallen disrepair   it's   a   story   I

heard a little about documented untold   we were taken

to the bridge group of cambridge undergraduates certainly

don't remember   seeing any women   rumour goes

it was the ladies of the night   siren   the bridge cannot

remember seeing   we thought we were pioneers no trace no

photographs no history   except from the story kept alive

  jane changes her job until a few months ago I was carrying

on with my peacetime   office phone   in newspaper it

said give us the bombs and planes we want

  employment exchange the same day   anything as a women

  with great confidence girls have taken on   enable

schedule   I took a job that a man   as soon as the men

came back I'd have something less   nowadays done by

women even operate   very posh   under the plough

    girls doing engineering lady platt aeronautical engineer

factory blacked out   see the look in their eyes answering the pilot in the advertisement helping to give him to be done

properly   nothing   about   building   nothing   about

construction   leave out construction industry   carried

on women supplemented the men   disappeared   over

night   say   we've   had   to   use   women   for   god   sake

   thousands 1941 temporary basis   insisted   they   were

paid far less   nothing that a woman can't do this is a salute

to women   I'd   look   down   and   my   trousers   would   be

alight edith moss welder   by 1944 there   were   nearly   25,000

women working in construction   strategic   absolute

censorship   standing there saying look at what we've done

   company   went   into   liquidation   thrown   in   skips

   keepsake that there were women   anecdotally   the

name of a particular lady was given to me I remember that but

not her name I will proceed to cut the ribbon still on timber

when the war began fortunate men who built the bridge   a

man's   world   I've   been   on   the   thames   all   my   life   65%

women's labour some say 90 newspaper over 70   I   say   this

was built by the ladies of london and I'm surprised it's still

standing and I usually get a few boos   it   was   so   hush   jane hyldon welder   I was no distance   certainly didn't know

it was not broadcast   was a story it was an urban myth

want to find a cash of letters or a woman still alive   tell   her

story   manual work unlikely that women had the energy

barrels full of concrete in conditions are they really going

to go home and write a diary   doubt   tourists

she came into the factory 14 years of age and they called her

whippet   got nice generous curves on it because ladies

built   I presume that you've tried the internet

my father used a crane I remember seeing ladies there

were lots of them   blue overalls   ladies did the lifting

and the tugging   all-in-one a bit similar to the men

they were quiet daddy used women   the women who did

help they didn't look like ladies in a flat cap   do you have

any memories   we weren't put down as the little women

we were the same as the chaps

I was making parts to go in that corner I started it the men

wanted their jobs back   get back to a happy normal family

life

he expected

so did the government   I hated that man because I loved
that job

they wanted to build the new britain

they wanted to help but it didn't happen

nah nah you never done it   8 years later   but   she
found photos of women dismantling the old   I can't believe
there wasn't a person who walked along with mum aunt
granny

who patted the bridge and said   bbc
spotlight the role official   named only as Dorothy

a few sentences if it means

role played will be recognised

via mother

queen   philippa   t-imber leaks   with every   t-ide of
the keel   every   t-ide leaks quarters
leaks   collect this new   t-ide with   every bin bag
philippa   bumps t-imber wets t-imber   with   hovis
factory wet   hair   with every t-ide   take to kings
road to   public baths to bring back
        special brew won't eat the rats   leak the rats
        or every t-ide homeopathic captains quarters shit
straight   into every t-ide   with every t-imber
        philippa leaks a cat   named z no   locks
with   every t-ide

via property

                                    leaving this
                                    open
                                    rent
                                    pocket of
                                    narrowing
                                            1-
                                    bedroom 1-
                                    bathroom
                                    juliette
                                    balcony
                                    inhale
                                            colne
                                    feeding the
                                    bigger

                                            pictu
                                    re   sent
                                    to   brother
                                    for
                                            appr
                                    oval   a
                                    studio with
                                    a
                                            view
                                    isleing

                                            the
                                    two rivers

                                    figure a

                                    rabbit

drowning
this   water
pressure

   chain

as   the
monsoon
is stuck on
full power

via library

to   the river

record   thames is probably a hyper object

to   bringing about the end   of   the concept
document   of   the world

to   part of   the bigger hyperobject of
to   the water

archive   the bridge
                                            cycle is the water
to   could Dorothy anticipate
to
t
collate   inside the human body
ttt   part   of
to   this hyperobject

research tt   turning
                                            the ignition is part
to   of   the hyperobject what
to t
tt   ttttttt   t   about welding or to engineer
                                                    tree – paved
to consider

                                            one week of warming

via 38 degrees

press ice block against   chest thigh   back
face wrap

tea towel   press against   chest   face
notice sweat   press   against   back   press
against   ribs   until   chest   face   sweat   press
against

block against   chest thigh   back thigh

tea towel   press against   damp   or
sweat

back   thigh press

                 against

against

grateful   you are not   at work   not
        on this construction site not
    layered in

    PPE

    not building this

                             bridge

via poem continued

from her
      layered   the wave
those waves
                                        waves constant
constantly drip from wave
from wave clothing those waves drip
      strain   constantly drips waves the wave drips
t   the wave is constant the drip from her
clothing wave dripping those waves
   ttt t   ttt   those drips the constant
her constant drip
those waves
      into   t   wave the
constant wave
constant from her
clothing drip waves drip
      corner   drip constant clothing constant
 her clothing the drip constantly drips
from her clothing to wave the drip drip
clothing the drip the wave clothes
her clothes drip clothing the   t   ttt
      remain   drip is constant
the those
                cleft t t t tt t   wave the
drip wave
the t the wave the
constant wave drips from
clothing her clothe the wave the drip
her the constant from her waving the
clothing waving her drip the wave
constant from the drip the
     t   through   clothing those
t waves those
constant from her

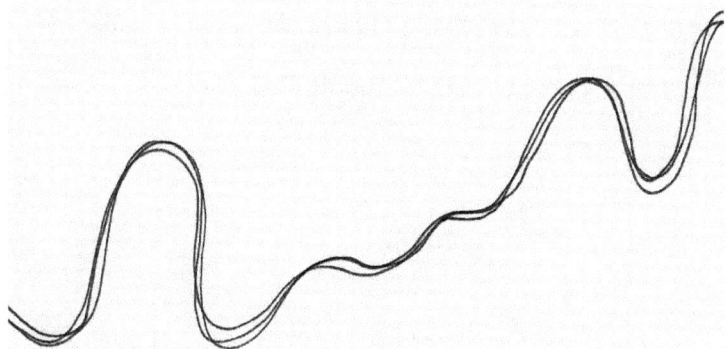

Sources

via poem: The Bridge of Sighs by Thomas Hood

via film: British Pathé, Reuters, Waterloo Bridge Construction Goes on (1942)

via photograph: Dorothy, National Science & Media Museum

via transcription: The Ladies' Bridge Documentary by Jo Wiser & Karen Livesey

via mother: Queen Philippa Houseboat, Albion Wharf

via library: Hyperobjects by Timothy Morton

Acknowledgements

Thank you to my wonderful family, in particular my Mum, Colette Stacey, who has always provided endless love and support.

Thank you to all of my wonderful teachers at Royal Holloway University, including Redell Olsen, Robert Hampson, Nisha Ramayya and Prue Bussey-Chamberlain. A special thanks to Dell, who has offered so much kindness, support, generosity, and time.

Thank you to my Poetic Practice course mates, fellow Crested Tits, and wonderful friends - Cat Chong, Emma Jenkins, Sophie Shepherd, Martina Krajňáková and Tiffany Charrington.

Thank you to Royal Holloway poetics students (past and present) including Karen Sandhu, Sarah Cave, Astra Papachristdoulou, JD Howse, Sarah Dawson, Rowan Evans, Chloe Proctor, Caroline Harris, Ariana Benson, Frances Uhomoibhi and Tanicia Pratt.

I would like to express my gratitude to JD Howse and Sarah Dawson from 'Theatre of Failure'; Allen Fisher, Valerie Soar and Charles Bernstein of 'King's Underground: Eric Mottram and spheres of contexts'; and David Dykes and Bethany Goodwill of 'Big Trouble!'. All of whom provided spaces where *Dorothy* was read in its various draft forms.

Thank you to Jackie Druiff and Emma Plant of Coombeshead Academy for inspiring my love of writing.

Thank you to my lovely colleagues and friends at Building Relations PR for supporting me throughout this project - Emily Coombes, Hollie Moore, Roseanna Lane, Katie Herbert, Emma Halford, Rachel Colgan, Kathryn Reucroft, Sreeja Karanam, Naomi Jackson, Kerry Chadwick, Ettie Long, Philippa Pinkerton, and Natasha Ley.

Thank you to my wonderful editor Aaron Kent for believing in this project.

Finally, the biggest thank you of all to my beautiful girlfriend Laura Hellon, and to Honey the bunny.

LAY OUT YOUR UNREST

www.ingramcontent.com/pod-product-compliance
Lightning Source LLC
Chambersburg PA
CBHW050950030426
42339CB00007B/369